D1206674

INVALIDES

Musée de l'Armée

The Hôtel des Invalides and Napoleon's Tomb

PARIS musées ■ Musée de l'Armée

Musée de l'Armée
Art et Histoire

List of authors

Christine Helfrich

*Curator of the Department
of Cultural Activities and Music*

Frédéric Lacaille

*Curator of the Department of Paintings
and Sculptures*

François Lagrange

Head of the Pedagogical Service

Jean-Pierre Reverseau

*Curator in Chief, Antique Department,
Arms and Armour*

> "Were I a prince, having founded this establishment would
> mean as much to me as having won three battles."
> Montesquieu[1]

In 1571, a century prior to the building of the Hôtel des Invalides, Maréchal de Montluc told the King of France, "Sire, you who are destined for great things, one of your principle concerns should be to establish a home for the poor wounded and disabled soldiers, as much to care for their injuries as to answer their needs... ...Sire, in honor of God, take care of the poor soldiers who lose arms and legs."

The echo of this stirring call is found in the edict founding the building when, in 1670, Louis XIV, judging it "nonetheless worthy of [his] pity than of [his] justice to keep these poor officers and soldiers from misery and mendacity", decided to establish "a royal hotel of grandeur and spaciousness, capable of receiving and lodging all officers and soldiers, whether old and invalid or disabled, and to endow it with sufficient funds for their subsistence."

Truly the symbol of the social thought of his century where, in Montesquieu's words, "the hand of a great monarch" is active everywhere, this chef d'œuvre of French classicism was widely admired and a source of inspiration for many sovereigns of foreign states.

Perhaps the greatest homage to the Hôtel des Invalides is that of its most famous occupant, Napoleon I, who no doubt thought of this institution, the object of all his attention, when he wrote in his last will and testament: *"I wish that my remains lie on the banks of the Seine, among the French people, whom I have loved so much."*

And so for three centuries, the Hôtel des Invalides, whose sober elegance stands out in the heart of Paris, has remained one of the most remarkable signatures of the 17th century, maintaining its primary mission while sheltering beneath its majestic gilded dome one of history's most illustrious figures as well as one of the finest collections of military heritage in the world.

We hope this book will be the most efficient of guides that may further an understanding of this magnificent monument which was the scene of so many events that have marked the history of our country.

Le Général de corps d'armée (2S) Bernard Devaux
Director of the Musée de l'Armée

1. C. L. de Montesquieu, *Lettres persanes,* Cologne, 1721, LXXXII.

ETABLISSEMENT
DE L'HOSTEL ROYAL
DES INVALIDES
1674

History of the Hôtel des Invalides

The Hôtel des Invalides is one of the most famous monuments of Paris. Its celebrity is due to the presence of the tomb of the Emperor Napoleon I in the Church of the Dome, as well as the majestic beauty of the architectural ensemble, most of it built during the reign of Louis XIV. Moreover, since the 19th century, the Hôtel des Invalides has housed within its several museums one of the oldest, most beautiful, and richest collections of objects related to the history and military heritage of France ever offered to the public.

Louis XIV's creation of the royal Hôtel des Invalides constitutes a great achievement of a reign that was exceptional in every way. Later on, Napoleon, the master politician, was fully aware of the importance of this achievement. Seconding the intentions of the Great King, Napoleon increased the Hôtel's funding, extended the privileges of its residents, and gave the Invalides a new dimension, that of a pantheon of military glory.

But who, among its many visitors, realizes that the original vocation of the Invalides has endured, through the Institution Nationale des Invalides, its ninety resident charges, and its ultra-modern medico-surgical complex?

The Noble Idea of a Reign

After the Treaty of the Pyrenees of November 7, 1659, had re-established peace in his states, Louis XIV set himself to contemplating the status of his veteran soldiers. Finding them a home became one of his priorities. Believing it only just that those who have risked their lives and sacrificed their blood in the service of the King should have a deserved rest, the sovereign was also conscious of the fact that nothing discourages a man from taking up the vocation of arms more effectively than the precarious condition of old soldiers. Earlier rulers had thought to resolve this question by turning the responsibility for invalid soldiers no longer fit for active service over to religious communities who would house and feed them. The number of these new recruits the abbeys and monasteries were obliged to care for, considered as oblates or lay monks, increased during the wars of Religion. Conscious of the difficult situation of invalid war veterans, in 1633, Louis XIII

The Hôtel des Invalides, during construction

Adam Pérelle
(1638-1695)
Etching and engraving
ca. 1680

Musée de l'Armée, Paris

The Siege of Cambrai, 22 March-6 April 1677
Mural in the Salle François Ier, one of four refectories for the invalid soldiers, 1679-1681

Joseph Parrocel (1646-1704)

had commissioned Cardinal Richelieu to establish the commander's residence of Saint-Louis at the site of the former château of Bicêtre. But the project foundered, for lack of funds. It was during Louis XIV's reign, following the War of Devolution, that the plan for the establishment of the Invalides took shape, in 1670. In January, the King transformed the obligation to receive veterans into a tax. The resultant funds were to support the subsistence of retired military men *"in a residence His Majesty has decided to build immediately, for this purpose"*. On April 15, 1670, Louis XIV announced his intention to rent a great house in Paris, in the faubourg Saint-Germain. By October 1st, the invalids were assembled for the first time in a building in the rue du Cherche-Midi. But, in a very short time it became evident that it lacked sufficient capacity to house them all.

An Establishment Inspired by Royal Will

The creation of the Hôtel des Invalides was part of a course of action aimed at the promotion of a new social stability. To establish it and give it form, Louis XIV chose a site at the plain of Grenelle, on the outskirts of Paris, and charged Louvois, his Minister of War, with the responsibility of implementing the project. Work began immediately. The King favored the plan submitted by the architect Libéral Bruant, who had already been commissioned to build the chapel of the hospital of Salpêtrière.

Founding of the Hôtel royal des Invalides, 1674
Pierre Dulin (1669-1748)
Oil on canvas, 1710-1715

Musée de l'Armée, Paris

A detailed program was submitted to the king, and estimates for the masonry were signed on March 14, 1671. The foundation stone was laid the following November 30th. The contract for the roofing and structural work was signed on February 11, 1673. In April, 1674, the edict of foundation states that the Hôtel is *"much advanced and almost in a state to house the said cripples"*. The first residents, for the most part survivors of the wars of Louis XIII, moved in to the new building in October, 1674, and were welcomed by Louis XIV. Since the Hôtel did not yet have a church, mass was temporarily celebrated in the grand salon (now the Salon d'honneur). However, at this stage of construction, Libéral Bruant hesitated. His repeated absences exasperated Louvois, and his incapacity to propose a satisfactory blueprint for the church slowed the work down considerably, to the degree that the minister asked another architect, Jules Hardouin-Mansart, grand-nephew by marriage of the famous François Mansart, to visit the construction site on March 14, 1676. On the 8th of April, the Minister of War commissioned him to complete the construction.

Detail:

Louvois, Minerva, and Architecture present Louis XIV with the blueprints for the hôtel. The painting blends allegory and history and brings together distinct events covering several years: the founding of the hôtel and approval of the blueprints (1670-1674), the construction of the hôtel (1671-1678) and the completion of the Dome (1706).

Barracks, Hospice, and Monastery

Detail:

Sentinel mounting the guard at meal time

Detail:

The water drinkers' table, those punished for failing to respect the rules of the hôtel are seated at the center.

The Hôtel was at once a barracks, where retired soldiers could participate in the controlled exercise of arms, a hospital, since medical care was available, and a hospice for officers and enlisted men who had no resources or were too old to support themselves.

The quadrangular plan behind the long facade, designed by Libéral Bruant, shows the influence of the layout of schools and other hospitals, edifices being built at that time to receive large communities. The residences, refectories, and areas designated for various activities were organized around different courtyards, and the ensemble was dominated by a chapel. This pattern was also the blueprint for the hospitals of La Salpêtrière in Paris and La Charité in Lyon.

Detail:

Sword-wearing soldiers of the guard are seated at the end of the table, near the entryway.

View of one of the refectories of the Hôtel des Invalides, around 1680-1681
Each of the refectories seated up to 400 soldiers at one serving.

Jean Lepautre (1618-1682)
Etching and engraving, ca. 1680-1681

Musée de l'Armée, Paris

At the Invalides, the church for the soldiers was complemented by a royal chapel with a cupola whose design resembles that of the Bourbon funerary chapel of the apse of the Basilica of Saint-Denis, conceived by François Mansart, which was never actually built.

The official inauguration of the church took place with pomp and ceremony on August 28, 1706. Work was resumed when the success of the Dutch Wars made it apparent that peace was near, and the Soldiers' Church was completed in 1678, according to Bruant's plans that had been revised by Hardouin-Mansart. Although the contracts for the foundation for the two churches were signed only a few months apart, the royal church was only completed thirty years later.

The Admission of Residents

*Invalid soldiers
at drill before the
façade of the hotel*

Anonymous
Gouache on paper,
ca. 1700

Musée de l'Armée,
Paris

Despite architectural and financial problems,
the Hôtel des Invalides has fulfilled its mission
since 1674.

Conditions for admission were strict, requiring
at least ten years of service, unless the candidate
could demonstrate that he was *"absolutely
incapable of service, either due to his advanced
age or incapacity, or due to wounds or incurable
illness"*.

Originally conceived to receive 1500 residents, the Hôtel was soon overwhelmed by their number.

And so, conditions of access became even more draconian. In 1710, for example, at least twenty years of uninterrupted military service were required, as well as an incurable disability.

Following pages:

Louis XIV arriving at the Invalides for the inauguration of the Church of the Dome, August 28, 1706

Pierre-Denis Martin (1663-1742)
Oil on canvas, ca. 1706
Musée Carnavalet, Paris

The Infirmary of the "Sœurs Grises"

The state of health of the war wounded was the object of particular concern. At the Invalides, the installation of vast infirmaries with modern equipment was evidently a priority. The space accorded them represents about a quarter of the surface of the Hôtel, on the ground floor and on the second story. Located in the southeast, the sickrooms were disposed in a pattern resembling a Greek cross around an altar where daily mass was celebrated. With three hundred beds equipped with curtains, for the first time, the bedridden were entitled to relative privacy. At Louis XIV's orders, Louvois requested the Filles de la Charité of the faubourg Saint-Lazare (nicknamed the "Sœurs grises") to take on the responsibility for the care of the patients, *"complete control of pharmaceutical supplies",* and the maintenance of the infirmaries. The thirty-seven Filles de la Charité had a predominant role, even in matters of pharmacy. The head pharmacist, or apothecary, as he was known at the time, was only entitled to prepare the most delicate of medicinal formulae. This can be interpreted as an attempt to end the abuse and trafficking common among apothecaries of military hospitals and private suppliers, all of them eager to make an extra profit from their assigned duties.

Far from such erring ways, one individual stood out in the 18th century due to the originality of his research. After passing the examination as a master apothecary in 1766, Antoine Parmentier worked at his official tasks during the day and, at night, devoted himself to his own work on the cultivation of the potato,

Detail:

Sister of Charity of the Order of Saint-Vincent-de-Paul. She wears the "cornet", the traditional head-dress characteristic of the Order.

Napoleon I visiting the infirmary of the Hôtel des Invalides, February 11, 1808

Alexandre Véron-Bellecour (1773-after 1838)
Oil on canvas, 1809

Musée national du château, Versailles

whose nutritional qualities he noticed while a prisoner in Prussia during the Seven Years War. His treatise on the tuber and its role in case of famine won him the prize of the Académie de Besançon in 1771 and the promotion to the post of head apothecary of the Invalides. The sisters would not allow him to take advantage of this title, but the scientist nonetheless continued with his philanthropic work, both in his laboratory at the Invalides and, first, in a little kitchen garden next to the Church of the Dome and then in a larger terrain granted him at the plain of Sablons, in Neuilly. Also acting under the authority of the Sœurs grises, the doctor and the officiating surgeon of the Hôtel both enjoyed a privileged status. The former was considered the family doctor of the king and profited from the favors and the honors this title conferred. The latter was entitled to train directly at the Invalides, in contact with the wounded, in the context of a mission of six years that was intended to spare him the corporatism common in his profession. The position of head surgeon, chosen among the most qualified practitioners, was created only in 1707.

Strict Internal Regulations

The religious organisation was strict. The priests of the congregation of the mission were expected to see to the religious instruction and salvation of the residents. As soon as he arrived at the Hôtel, the soldier was restricted from any outings during forty days, the time devoted to this instruction. First twelve, then twenty, the priests were housed at the west of the Soldiers' Church, on three floors.

Daily life was all the more austere since discipline and very strict rules left the residents with little liberty. The enlisted men shared rooms of four or six, and the officers were placed by twos or threes in rooms that, contrary to those of simple soldiers, were heated. All of them were expected to keep their rooms clean and not to store any food, wine, or tobacco, the sale of which was forbidden, there. The internal regulations tolerated no misconduct, sanctions ranging from being strapped to a wooden horse in public, to internment in prison, to being sent to the hospice of Bicêtre and even expelled from the Hôtel without any pension, depending upon the nature of the misdeed. The officers were free to circulate within the Hôtel and to leave the

Uniforms of the disabled, 1786: regular companies, companies on special detachment, officer

Alfred de Marbot (1812-1865) and Alexandre David (active around 1828-1856)
Lithograph, 1845

Musée de l'Armée, Paris

The Baron d'Espagnac, Governor of the Hôtel, granting an invalid pardon, ca. 1770-1780.

After a drawing by Boulay (active during the 18th century)

Musée de l'Armée, Paris

premises at will, but the lower ranks and enlisted soldiers had to be dressed in uniform and possess a pass signed by the governor. These strict regulations were enforced by military supervision under the authority of the governor. The residents were organised in companies and assigned guard duty and drills under the command of a captain. Their attire consisted of a woollen uniform, without lapels, and breeches of the same material, worn for parades and when they were outside the Hôtel. Within the confines of the residence, they wore only a simple jacket of yellow leather. In 1775, a black, felt, wide-brimmed hat without braid, the brim turned up on the right side, was added to complete the outfit.

Work was encouraged during the week, in their rooms and, later, in the workshops. The healthiest among them were sent on detachment to fortified towns.

The Workshops

Below:

Gradual and Antiphony for use at the Hôtel royal de Saint-Louis des Invalides (frontispiece)

Atelier of illuminated manuscripts of the Invalides
Gouache with gold accents, on parchment, 1682

Musée de l'Armée, Paris

A cobbler existed at the hôtel, probably as early as 1676. There were also tapestry weavers (approved up until 1696) and tailors, who did an increasing business. Situated on the fourth floor of the wings lining the main courtyard, the workshops were run by professionals in each domain, rapidly seconded by the most deft and experienced residents.

This flurry of activity provoked the hostility of the craftsmen's corporations, who were not entitled to the same tax exemptions on the purchase of raw materials. If the tapestries woven at the Invalides which decorate the Salle du Conseil (now the Salon d'Honneur) and the Church of Saint-Louis are known for their fine quality, the illuminated manuscripts and liturgical works are just as remarkable. The studio of illumination employed the invalids, and Louis XIV, impressed with their work when he visited there, commissioned liturgical books for the chapel at Versailles. The gradual and antiphony made for the Invalides and completed in 1682, illustrated with vignettes, decorative foliage, frontispieces and full page polychromes, is reminiscent of the traditions of monastic illuminated manuscripts. Since there are other works marked with the insignia « *made at the Hôtel des Invalides* », it is probable that the artists of calligraphy and illumination also worked for private individuals and for religious communities. The collective activities of the factories and workshops apparently ceased after the death of Louis XIV.

Opposite:

Plainsong for the Feast of the Ascension
Page of the gradual and antiphony [...]

Musée de l'Armée, Paris

24

ia. Com. Sállite Dó-

mino, qui ascendit su per

cæ los cæ ló rum ad o-

rien tem al le -

lú ia. I.

The Supervision of a Legacy

The success of the Invalides continued into the 18th century, but the number of residents raised some delicate problems of management. Beginning in the reign of Louis XV, the Hôtel adopted a policy aimed at limiting admissions and encouraging invalids to leave the establishment. Those residents deemed still apt for service were sent to frontier posts and integrated into detachment companies. The Duc de Choiseul, Minister of War until 1770, wanted the Hôtel to be exclusively reserved for the cripples, invalids, and « *caducs* ». Under the influence of the Comte de Saint-Germain, the new Minister of War, a decree of June 17, 1776, reduced the number of residents to 1500.

The Invalides and the Revolution

On the morning of July 14, 1789, a crowd of excited Parisians came to the Invalides in search of weapons. Taken by assault, the iron gates gave way and several thousand rifles and twenty-seven cannons were seized, the governor, the Marquis de Sombreuil, incapable of the slightest resistance. By a decree of April 30, 1791, the National Assembly decided that the establishment formerly known as the Royal Hôtel of the Invalides would henceforth be called the "Hôtel national des militaires invalides" ("*National Hôtel of Invalid Soldiers*"). The National Treasury would provide for the institution and the maintenance of the Hôtel. The companies on detachment were abolished.

The people of Paris leaving the Invalides on the morning of July 14, 1789, having taken the arms stored there
The weapons confiscated by the frenzied crowd would serve to intimidate the guards of the Bastille.

Jean-Baptiste Lallemand (1716-1803)
Oil on canvas, ca. 1700

Musée Carnavalet, Paris

In 1794, everything related to royalty and religion was eliminated. The canopied main altar of the Church of the Dome, the effigies, *fleurs de lys* and royal emblems were destroyed, while the statues of the church were removed and abandoned on the esplanade. Now become the «Temple of Victory» and, later, the «Temple of Mars», the royal church hosted the *Feast of Concord* on July 14, 1800, celebrated in the presence of the Consuls, with the accompanying music from Etienne Méhul's *Chant du 25 messidor*. On September 22, 1800, the remains of Turenne, spared during the profanations of the Revolution at Saint-Denis, were received by the residents of the Invalides.

Detail:

Emperor Napoleon I
awards an invalid
his cross.

The Military Pantheon of France

From that time on, The Invalides took on a new
mission, that of a memorial and a pantheon of
military glory, placed under the protection of the
veterans of the Hôtel. Services were celebrated
anew in the church.

On July 15, 1804, the first awarding of decorations
of the members of the order of the Legion of Honor,
as well as the solemn oath of its members, took
place in a ceremony of pomp and grandeur.

As the choir sang Pierre Desvignes's *Te Deum,*
the Emperor honored Generals Kellermann and
Oudinot, scientists Monge, Parmentier and Jussieu,

First distribution of the crosses of the Legion of Honor in the Church of the Invalides, July 14, 1804

Jean-Baptiste Debret (1768-1848)
Oil on canvas, 1812

Musée national du château, Versailles

composers Méhul and Lesueur, artists David and Gérard, sculpter Houdon, and the gastronome Brillat-Savarin.

On May 17, 1807, Napoleon had the flags and standards captured at Iena hung beneath the dome, as well as the sword of Frederic II, King of Prussia, which he had taken at Potsdam. The invalids were charged with guarding the display. Returning to the basics of the founding Edict, a decree of March 25, 1811, placed the Hôtel under the direct authority of the Emperor, and the State set aside a substantial subsidy for it.

The Cult of the Emperor

After Waterloo, the establishment remained a fief and a sanctuary dedicated to the faithful preservation of the memory of the Emperor. Nicknamed «the den» (of Bonapartism) by the monarchists, it lost its financial autonomy during the Restoration.

It was Louis-Philippe who commanded the return of the Emperor's remains in a law of June 10, 1840, and he sent his own third son, the Prince de Joinville, to accomplish the task.

The Prince cast off from Toulon on July 7th, on the *Belle-Poule*, arriving at Saint Helena three months later. There, the Emperor's casket was exhumed and his body identified on the morning of October 15th, an extremely emotional scene, particularly for the old generals, Bertrand and Gourgaud, the faithful valet Marchand, the young Baron de Las Cases, and a few others who had accompanied Napoleon into exile twenty-five years before. The coffin was hauled up on a funereal chariot and driven to the ship, which cast off on October 18th.

The *Belle-Poule* returned to Cherbourg, arriving on November 30th. The Emperor's coffin was loaded on to a steamboat, the *Dorade*, which made a week-long journey up the Seine to Paris, accompanied by a flotilla and cheering crowds who shouted "Vive l'Empereur!" At Courbevoie, the casket left the ship and was loaded onto a triumphal chariot drawn by sixteen horses.

On December 15, 1840, in the midst of a substantial crowd, despite the biting cold, the

Napoleon I on the imperial throne

Jean-Auguste-Dominique Ingres (1780-1867)
Oil on canvas, 1806

Musée de l'Armée, Paris

Eagle, 1804 model

After Antoine-Denis Chaudet (1764-1810)
Gilded bronze

Musée de l'Armée, Paris

funereal chariot traversed Paris. After crossing the Etoile, it passed through the Arc de Triomphe, down the Champs Elysées to the Place de la Concorde, and over the Seine to the Left Bank.

At last it reached the Invalides, amidst an honor guard of colossal statues representing the kings and great captains of France, erected especially for the occasion. Carried to the main courtyard by the crew of the *Belle-Poule*, the casket was greeted by the clergy and taken into the Soldiers'Church. The altars had been disassembled to permit the passage of the casket all the way to the Church of the Dome, where it was placed on a catafalque sheltered by a dome supported by four columns and surmounted by an eagle, draped in white satin and heavy gold funeral hangings. The Church of the Dome itself was hung with purple velvet with a pattern of golden bees and eagles.

Shortly thereafter the casket was placed in the Chapel of Saint-Jérôme, where it remained until 1861, when it was definitively installed in the "crypt" designed by the architect Louis Visconti. Henceforth, the Church of the Dome became the mausoleum of the cult of the Emperor.

The Soldiers' Church remained reserved for the residents of the Hôtel. Today it is the headquarters of the curacy of the armies and serves as the setting of the funerals of some of the State's most distinguished servants and of military ceremonies, whereas the main courtyard is the chosen site of parades and military reviews.

Emperor Napoleon I's hat, worn at the Battle of Eylau

Poupard, hat maker Felt

Musée de l'Armée, Paris

Allegory of the *Return of the Remains of Napoleon I*

François Trichot Oil on canvas, 1846

Musée de l'Armée, Paris

The Assertion of the Vocation of Cultural Heritage

Right:

The Arms Magazine of the Arsenal, in Paris, 18th century
This arms depot was the partial source at the origin of the Musée d'Artillerie, first established in the convent of Saint-Thomas d'Aquin, in Paris, in 1796-1797, and then transferred to the Invalides after the war of 1870-1871.

Anonymous
Watercolor print,
18th century

Musée de l'Armée, Paris

During the second half of the 19th century, the original function of the Hôtel des Invalides as a hospital became less important while its patrimonial and administrative dimension expanded.

There were only nine hundred resident military veterans in 1864, while they had numbered three thousand in 1850, and by 1914, only seventeen remained. The hospital would vastly increase its activities when World War I began. But part of the site, particularly the refectories, progressively took on other functions.

The military administration moved into one part of the building. The military government of Paris left its offices at the Place Vendôme for the Hôtel in 1898. Still present there today, it shares the site with the Secrétariat général de la Défense nationale (SGDN), among others.

The Invalid Soldier, ca. 1815-1830
Under the Ancien Régime, a battery of cannons was installed at the north entry, where it remains today. Little by little, a number of trophies were added during the 19th century.

Hippolyte Bellangé
(1800-1866)
Lithography

Musée de l'Armée, Paris

The patrimonial vocation, long a part of the Hôtel's history, thenceforth developed. By the end of the 18th century, relief maps from the time of Vauban on, representing the fortifications of France's borders, were already installed in the attic. In 1793, the Church of the Dome was rechristened the "Temple of Mars and of warrior virtues", and soon the trophies of war were assembled at the Invalides. Flags and standards brought from Notre-Dame Cathedral were presented in the Soldiers' Church, and artillery pieces of several different origins were displayed at the entry to the Hôtel. With the installation of the Musée d'Artillerie in 1871, and then of the Musée historique de l'Armée in 1896, the image and the function of the Hôtel further evolved. The site was progressively transformed into one of the most important repositories of France's military heritage.

Following pages:

Visit of the Duc d'Angoulême to the Hôtel royal des Invalides, 17 January 1822
The prince is received in the southwestern refectory, now one of the rooms of the museum. In the tradition of royal visits to the hôtel, the prince asks to taste the wine of the Invalides.

Benoît-Benjamin Bonvoisin (1788-1860)
Oil on canvas,
Ca. 1823-1824

Musée de Beaux-Arts, Rouen

The Museums of the Invalides and the History of the Collections

As a result of both the edifice's past and the history of its different collections, the Invalides is presently the home of the Musée de l'Armée, as well as the Musée des Plans-reliefs and the Musée de l'Ordre de la Libération.

The Musée des Plans-reliefs

In 1668, Louis XIV commissioned a series of scale models representing the land and maritime fortresses of the kingdom. Produced by the most capable engineers of the times on a 1/600th scale, their purpose was to provide precise representations that would permit the implementation of an effective defense policy in case of conflict. In 1697, the collection was composed of 141 models, most of them then installed in the Grande Galerie of the Louvre. Given their strategic interest, a special authorization from the King was required to view them.

In the years 1776-1777, the beginning of work to refurbish the Louvre was the occasion for their transfer to the attic of the Invalides. The presence of these scale models is the oldest evidence of the patrimonial vocation of the Invalides.

Relief map of the
Hôtel des Invalides
Ca. 1679-1690
**Musée de l'Armée,
Paris**

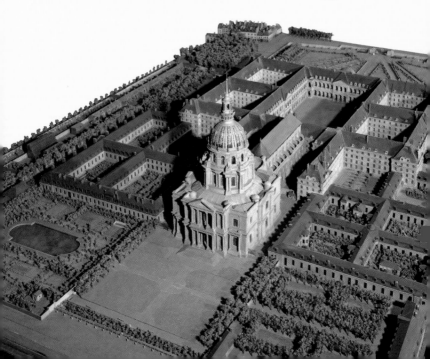

Small ornamental
cannon, a gift
to Louis XIV from
the parlement of
Franche-Comté

Laurent Ballard, 1676

**Musée de l'Armée,
Paris**

"Bourguignotte au
griffon"

**Giovan Paolo Negroli
(attributed to), Milan,
Ca. 1540-1545**

**Musée de l'Armée,
Paris**

Sword

Ca. 1350

**Musée de l'Armée,
Paris**

The Musée de l'Armée

The Musée de l'Armée (see p. 42)
is the result of the combination of
the Musée d'Artillerie and the Musée
historique de l'Armée, two separate
establishments of different origin,
in 1905.

• **The Musée d'Artillerie** was created
during the revolutionary era. In 1795,
it was housed in the former
Dominican-Jacobin convent of
Saint-Thomas-d'Aquin, in the faubourg
Saint-Germain, a "depot for models
of weaponry and of war machines".
The Artillery committee's safeguarding
action was similar to others in the
domain of beaux-arts and permitted
the conservation of a remarkable
collection of arms, armour, and military
memorabilia mentioned in an 1806
report to the Emperor as *"The most
precious collection of offensive and*

The Museums of the Invalides and the History of the Collections

defensive arms since those of the Savages [sic], dating up until those currently in use in various European countries." After the war of 1870-1871, lacking space at Saint-Thomas-d'Aquin, the museum transferred its collections to the Invalides, where they were placed in the west wing of the main courtyard.

• **The Musée historique de l'Armée** resulted from the retrospective military exhibit displayed on the esplanade of the Invalides during the Universal Exposition of 1889. The project for a permanent museum of the army, long demanded by a portion of the public, was supported by La Sabretache, a patriotic association headed by painters Ernest Meissonnier and Edouard Detaille. It took shape in 1896 with the installation of the collections in the east wing of the main courtyard, facing the rooms of the Musée d'Artillerie. Presenting the program of the new Musée historique de l'Armée, Général Billot, Minister of War observed that *"the French army was lacking a salle d'honneur perpetuating the traditions of its glorious past with the trophies of its former victories, with arms, flags, uniforms…."*

Dress uniform of a fife player of the Cent-Suisses

Ca. 1700

Musée de l'Armée, Paris (depot of the Musée national suisse, Zurich)

Breastplate of Carabiniere Fauveau, killed at Waterloo on June 18th, 1815
Musée de l'Armée, Paris

Verdun
Félix Vallotton (1865-1925)
Oil on canvas, 1917
Musée de l'Armée, Paris

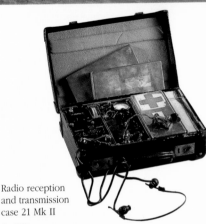

Radio reception and transmission case 21 Mk II
Ca. 1942
Musée de l'Armée, Paris

The Musée de l'Ordre de la Libération

In 1970, the Musée de l'Ordre de la Libération was opened in the southwest section of the Hôtel. It constitutes a memorial to the fighters of the order created by Général de Gaulle on November 16, 1940. Its mission is to leave a tangible trace of the Free French, the Resistance, and the Deportation through its collection of documents and memorabilia. It is supervised by the chancellery of the Ordre de la Libération (Ministry of Justice).

The Musée de l'Armée

The Musée de l'Armée, a public establishment of the Defense Ministry, displays collections that come from such divers areas as history and "militaria" (arms, armour, uniforms, emblems, artillery, historic memorabilia), archaeology, ethnography, the beaux-arts, science and technology, etc. They represent the largest collections of this kind belonging to the nation and are among the most famous in the world. They are arranged in several chronological groups—from medieval times to the present—and thematic ensembles.

The Renaissance is very amply represented by an impressive collection of arms and armour—the weapons chamber of the kings of France, jousting and tournament armour—which includes masterpieces

Standard of the 2nd Regiment of Dragoons, known as the "escaped standard", smuggled out of France clandestinely in 1943
Musée de l'Armée, Paris

from the principle European schools of gunsmiths and armorers. The greater part of the displays of firearms is devoted to hunting weapons. An Oriental collection, with pieces from the Near East, China, and Japan, provides a useful basis of comparison with European products. The ensemble of weapons, uniforms, emblems, historic souvenirs, etchings, and paintings recall the history of the French army and its campaigns, from the reign of Louis XIII until the end of the Second World War. The royal household and the Grande Armée of Napoleon I are particularly well represented in these

Armour of François Ier

Jörg Seusenhofer and Degen Pirger, Innsbruck, 1539-1540

Musée de l'Armée, Paris

collections. Many personal objects, including the uniform he wore at Marengo, one of his grey frock coats, several of his hats, and even his deathbed from Sainte-Hélène, evoke the memory of the Emperor himself. The museum contains the largest French collection of artillery pieces, full-sized pieces or small models, built to scale and used in the instruction of officers.

The space devoted to World War II, inaugurated in 2000, similarly presents the history of the war and the action of France Libre (the Free French). It constitutes the first phase of Project ATHENA. (The acronym stands for Armée, Tradition, Histoire, Emblèmes, Nation, Armement.)

Shield
France, ca. 1550
Musée de l'Armée, Paris

Renault G7 taxi, known as the « Taxi of the Marne »
Musée de l'Armée, Paris

ATHENA, a project for the modernisation of the Musée de l'Armée

The Musée de l'Armée is currently undergoing reorganisation and modernisation, in keeping with the ATHENA plan, supervised by the Defense Ministry, which should be completed in 2008.

Following the space devoted to the Second World War, opened in 2000, a new section of work involves the west wing and should open in 2005. It will contain arms and armour, from medieval times until the 1650s, on the ground floor, and, on the upper floors, the military history of France from 1871 to 1939. The subsequent phase will transform the east wing to house the collections from 1630 until the Franco-Prussian war of 1870-1871. The last part of the project will permit the presentation of several thematic ensembles, including artillery, cavalry, regulation weaponry, and emblems.

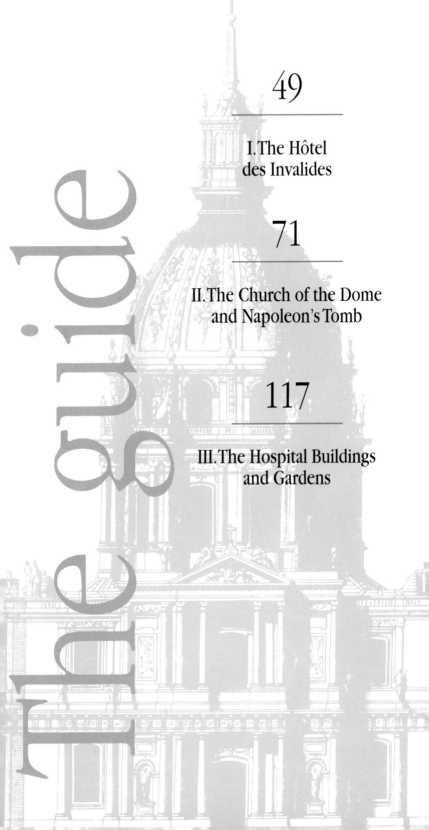

The guide

I.

The Hôtel des Invalides

The Hôtel des Invalides should be discovered from the banks of the Seine, at a far enough distance to see Jules Hardouin-Mansart's dome in all its great height that dominates the long, austere façade of Libéral Bruant. From this viewpoint one can measure the vastness of the edifice, the greatest architectural enterprise undertaken in Paris during the reign of Louis XIV, and judge the respective merits of the two architects successively responsible for its creation.

Once situated in the country, on the outskirts of Paris, at the edge of a faubourg Saint-Germain that was rapidly growing, the hôtel is surrounded by dry moats that emphasize its military vocation. Facing the esplanade and lining the moats, a group of cannons seems to challenge the visitor. Those that frame the iron grille of the entry, taken as trophies in military campaigns, constitute the «triumphal battery» which once, activated by the residents of the hôtel, resounded in the ears of all of Paris on grand occasions.

The facade

The facade, built by Libéral Bruant in 1671-1675 and firmly planted between two large, square pavilions, is 195 meters long (100 *toises*, [1 toise = 6 feet] in measurement standards of the times) and faces the Seine. It stands around the central design of an arch of triumph which encompasses the great entry portal and the three windows of the Salle du Conseil (the present day Salon d'honneur). The ensemble is extremely sober. The four stories of windows, marked vertically by a series of transeptual breaks, and horizontally by string courses and the prominent entablature separating the floors, are capped by a high roof bordered by ornamental flames and large lucarnes in the form of armour and, on the pavilions, large trophies of arms that surround a seated suit of armour.

The sculpted décor of the frontispiece was undertaken during the reign of Louis XIV. Both the arch embellished with chutes of trophies arranged about a radiant sun and the sculpted wood trim of the portal, designed by Mansart, date from this period

(around 1680). Cupids bearing helmets decorate the volets of the double doors, and a seated Minerva presents the coat of arms of France upon the tympan. Left unfinished for over half a century, this décor was completed in 1733-1734 by one of the most prominent artists of Louis XV's reign, Guillaume Coustou. He is responsible for the trophy and the head of Hercules that mark the arch over the entry as well as the imposing seated figures of Mars and Minerva that decorated the avant-corps (redone in 1966, since the originals were in a state of

North façade
of the Hôtel

extreme degradation). The former, the god of War, accompanied by a wolf, symbolizes the brute force of combat. The latter, the goddess of Wisdom, with an owl at her feet, represents the art of war, conducted with skill and reflection.

The pediment bears a great bas-relief showing Louis XIV, the founder of the hôtel, on horseback and dressed in a costume of Antiquity, upon a pedestal flanked by the seated virtues, Justice and Prudence. The Latin inscription may be translated as follows: *"Louis the Great, out of royal munif-*

icence for his soldiers and provident for times to come, founded this edifice in the year 1675." The figure of the king, which was disfigured by hammering during the Revolution, was restored in 1814-1816 by the sculptor Pierre Cartellier.

☞ Access to the main courtyard is through a vestibule with Ionic columns, originally flanked by the guardroom (which now serves as the reception area to the Musée de l'Armée) and a small armoury.

The avant-corps of the north façade

The Cour d'Honneur

The great courtyard of the hôtel–formerly the royal courtyard, today the main courtyard or *cour d'honneur*– is at the heart of the monument. It is about 102 meters long by 64 meters in width, and is lined with galleries of arcades on two stories that allow circulation with protection from the elements and extend through long corridors that cross the edifice.

The roof is bordered by pediments and ample lucarnes, richly sculpted with representations of trophies of arms that recall anew the military character of the place. Pairs of horses, trampling upon captives, adorn the corner pavilions.

The courtyard served as a commons in the daily life of the residents. The administrative services, the Salle du Conseil, and the governor's apartments and those of his officers were located near the north entry. The long sides, that is to say, on the east and the west, were flanked on the ground floor by the soldiers' refectories and, beyond, by the officers' mess and the kitchens and, upstairs, by the

The Cour d'honneur (main courtyard)

52

Above left:

Arcades and
lucarnes of the
Cour d'honneur

Above right:

Horses trampling
a prisoner.
sculpted group,
Cour d'honneur

Above:

This lucarne bears
the decorative
interpretation
of a traditional play
on words, where
a wolf (loup) peers
(voit) through
the reeds, a riddle
(«Loup voit»)
alluding to the
name of Louis XIV's
Minister of War,
Louvois, protector
of the Hôtel.

workshops and barracks. On the south side, a more elaborately decorated portico lent access to the Church of Saint-Louis.

The sundials on the pillars of the three avant-corps that face the sunlight were engraved in the 1770s, under the ministry of the Duc de Choiseul. They still tell accurate solar time and indicate a number of other things related to important dates for the life and the history of the hôtel and the feast of Saint Louis. Along with the chimes of the church clock, installed in the campanile in 1677 and 1786, their faces punctuated the residents' day. In the 19th century, an immense painted mural decorated the walls of the ground floor gallery. Commissioned from Bénédict Masson in 1864, it represented the military splendor of France during the reigns of Charlemagne, Saint Louis, Louis XIV and Napoleon I. Exposed to the weather, restored in 1913, it disappeared between the First and Second World War.

The scene of the exhibition of trophies–weapons, tanks, airplanes, matériel of all kinds–during the Great War, the courtyard and its galleries presently contain the better part of the Musée de l'Armée's collection of artillery pieces.

North porch of the Cour d'honneur, with sundials upon the pillars

Above:

East porch of the Cour d'honneur, one of the entrances to the Musée de l'Armée

Below:

Classic French cannons (17th-18th centuries) before the west entry of the Musée de l'Armée

The Refectories

*(access to
the Musée de l'Armée)*

There are four refectories, situated at different areas of the Cour d'honneur in the east wing and in the west wing. In two services, they could accommodate the Hôtel's fifteen hundred residents for their daily meals. When the building was constructed, the mural décor of the refectories represented, in four sequences, the principle events of the War of Devolution (1667-1668) and the Dutch Wars. Every refectory had its own suite of mural compositions, introduced by and ending with paintings of the king, commander in chief, giving

orders for the campaign and accepting the surrender of the enemy. The walls facing the windows bore landscapes, as though opening on to the countryside with a view of the Flemish and Dutch cities the royal armies had conquered.

Jacques Friquet de Vauroze painted the murals in the east wing and Michel II Corneille, Etienne Allegrain, and Joseph Parrocel collaborated to produce those in the west wing, all between 1678 and 1681. Today, the refectories mark the access to the Musée de l'Armée and also contain some of its collections.

Below:

Murals depicting battles decorate the refectories which serve, today, as rooms of the Musée de l'Armée

Jacques Friquet de Vauroze (1648-1716)
Oil on plaster, 1678
Southeast refectory

Opposite:

Detail of
The Capture of Tournai, 21-25 June 1667

Jacques Friquet de Vauroze, (1648-1716)
Oil on plaster, 1678
Northeast refectory

The Galleries

☞ The two great staircases on either side of the Church of Saint-Louis, at the south end of the courtyard, lend access to the galleries on each floor. Residents' bedrooms opened directly on to the galleries or on to the corridors that were closed with a simple iron grille.

In the northwest corner, on the second floor, graffiti depicting shoes scar the pillars, a reminder of one of the principle activities of the workshops of the hôtel, the fabrication of clothing and shoes for the soldiers of the royal armies. The arched form of the shoes, with the heel slanted towards the front, dates these drawings to the end of the reign of Louis XIV, shortly after the completion of the hotel.

Below:

Wrought-ironwork of one of the stairways of the Cour d'honneur

Above:
Graffiti of a shoe, end of the 17th-beginning of the 18th century, on one of the pillars of the upper story of the Cour d'honneur

Opposite:
View of the upper story of the east gallery, showing chamber doors

The Salon
d'honneur

Louis XIV,
after Hyacinthe
Rigaud.
Replica of
the celebrated
portrait (1701,
musée du
Louvre, Paris)
donated to
the Hôtel by
Louis XVIII
in 1823

**Musée de l'Armée,
Paris**

The Salon d'Honneur

(reserved access)

At the middle of the north gallery, three great windows open on to the Salon d'honneur, the former Salle du Conseil of the establishment. This immense room offers a broad and open view of the Seine. It served temporarily as a chapel during construction work on the church before it was designated as the site of conferences and receptions of the governor of the hôtel. This room housed the library of the hôtel from 1800 to 1877 and was restored in 1918, and once again in 1974. The interior décor, most of it dating from the era of Louis XIV, includes high doors capped by radiant suns supported by pairs of lions couchants and a large cornice decorated with trophies. The narrow, rococo panels that frame the hearth, added in 1734, are the work of sculptor and *ornemaniste* Jacques Verberckt.

After the First World War, the walls and the vault of the salon were refurbished in a painted décor whose themes would celebrate the great moments of glory in the defense of the nation. Begun by François Flameng and completed by his pupil Charles Hoffbauer at the end of the 1930s, it was removed during the Second World War. The displays of weaponry and the paintings that decorate this room today belong to the collections of the Musée de l'Armée.

☞ Going back down, one arrives at the south gallery of the courtyard, wider than the others, that serves as the covered square of the Church of Saint-Louis des Invalides, also called the Soldiers'Church.

The radiant sun, symbol of King Louis XIV

Above the door of the Salon d'honneur

Saint-Louis or the Soldiers' Church

The Church of Saint-Louis was built to accommodate the residents of the Hôtel for the celebration of daily mass. Lacking a transept, it has a

Trophies on the vault of the Soldiers'Church (detail)

Opposite:

The Soldiers' Church, nave and choir. At the far end, the window that separates the church from the Church of the Dome since 1872-1873.

Alexandre Thierry, was seriously damaged by the explosion of the munitions depot of Grenelle at the end of the 18th century and was subject to several unfortunate restorations before it was finally rebuilt in its entirety between 1955 and 1957 in the neo-classical style.

The bronze balustrade that marks the entry to the nave, which once served as a communion table at the entry to the choir, and the white marble pulpit, embellished with gilded bronze bas reliefs, were added during the First Empire and the Restoration, respectively.

well-lit nave and a barrel vault with nine bays whose semi-circular archways open on to the aisles. These are surmounted by galleries that look out on the nave through basket-handle arches. The bays are separated by pilasters capped by Corinthian capitals.

• *The furnishings*

The organ case (see p. 65), fashioned between 1679 and 1687 by Germain Pilon, regular carpenter of the King's Buildings, has five turrets supported by figures of Atlas and decorated with cherubs. The instrument, crafted by the king's organ builder,

• *The trophies*

The flags and standards taken from the enemy, suspended over the galleries, belong to an ancient tradition.

Ever since the reign of Louis XIII, the trophies had been carried by the Swiss Guard to Notre Dame de Paris where they were hung beneath the vault. During the Convention, in 1793, they were transferred to the Invalides. Henceforth, the invalids themselves were the recipients of the symbols of France's victories. Thus, on the 20 Pluviôse of the year VIII (February 9, 1800), the flags taken from the enemy by Bonaparte's army of the

Orient were presented by Général Lannes to Minister of War Carnot and placed in "this temple of warrior virtues".

In 1814, there were 1417 flags in the church. The overflow was such that a platform was built under the organ stand to hold those the nave could no longer contain. But on March 30, 1814, the Minister of War ordered Maréchal Sérurier, Governor of the Invalides, to protect the precious trophies from the enemy marching on Paris. As he could not evacuate them, Sérurier was compelled to have them burned on a bonfire built in the main courtyard, according to the laws of war. The ashes were thrown in the Seine.

The tradition of military trophies has, nonetheless, been carried on for over one hundred twenty years, in all the conflicts in which France has engaged.

The Governors' crypt

• *The governors' crypt*

(access reserved)

Built beneath the Soldiers' Church, it was initially designated as the burial place of the governors of the Hôtel. Since the 19th century, it has also sheltered the tombs of great military figures. Several marshals of France–Pélissier, MacMahon, Fayolle, Maunoury, Juin, and Leclerc–lie in repose next to Baron Larrey, head surgeon of the Grande Armée, and Rouget de Lisle, author of the *Marseillaise*.

☞ Two corridors form the passage between the main courtyard and the south section of the Hôtel, where the Church of the Dome is located.

Heroic Music
and Funereal Dirges

The organ case

Saint-Louis des Invalides is not an ordinary parish. Many official ceremonies are held here, and its vaults have always rung with the notes of the most solemn airs.

Delalande's *Te Deum* was played when the king officially inaugurated the new church on August 28, 1706. Ever since then, every important event has been celebrated there with music, whether the convalescence of Louis XV (1744), or the coronation of Louis XVI (1775). Both were the occasion of a *Te Deum* accompanied by resounding trumpets and timpani and gun salutes of cannon and musket. This was also the site of great revolutionary celebrations

that included hundreds of instrumentalists and choristers gathered together in several orchestras and choirs arranged throughout the church.

Berlioz's *Messe des Morts*, played for the first time at the Invalides on December 5, 1837, during the funeral service for de Damrémont, was accompanied by heroic singing offset by a background of artillery salvos.

For the December 15, 1840, Return of the Remains of Napoleon, *Mozart's Requiem* was chosen to accompany a production whose tone was at once funereal and triumphant.

Saint-Louis des Invalides:
One Church or Two?

The visitor notices the difference in style and dimension between the "Church of the Dome", or "royal church", and the "Soldiers' Church". Still, Saint-Louis is the patron saint of both, and both can be designated by the name "Saint-Louis des Invalides". Moreover, if we study simply the blueprints of the two churches, we realise that they share a spatial continuity and, in fact, virtually form one immense church, with the Soldiers' Church serving as the nave and the Church of the Dome as the choir and transept.

Still, from the time of their creation during the reign of Louis XIV, the Church of the Dome and the Soldiers' Church constituted two distinct entities, separated rather than united by a double altar: on the north, the Soldiers' Church, reserved for residents of the hôtel, opens on to the main courtyard, and at the south, the grandiose royal chapel.

Religious services, abolished by the Revolution, were reinstated by the First Consul, Napoleon Bonaparte. Once he had become emperor, he intended to use the two churches as one ensemble, as was the case for the grand ceremony for the members of the Legion of Honor on July 15, 1804.

But the experiment was not conclusive, and after lengthy consideration, Napoleon gave up the idea of holding his coronation ceremony at the Invalides.

The Consulate and the Empire introduced an important functional distinction between the two churches. The Church of the Dome began its transformation into a military pantheon when it welcomed the funeral monument of Vauban and the tomb of Turenne, whereas, once religious services were re-established, the Soldiers' Church returned to its traditional mission as a church for invalid soldiers.

The edification of the monumental tomb of Napoleon in the Church of the Dome beginning in 1841-1842 heralded the clear separation of the two churches, and there was no longer any real communication between the Church of the Dome, which had become the mausoleum of Napoleon, and the Soldiers' Church. The definitive separation of the two churches was marked by a huge window, installed in 1872-1873 by the architect Crépinet.

Above right:

Scale model of the Church of the Dome, revealing the connection with the Soldiers' Church.

Philippe Velu, 1997

Musée de l'Armée, Paris

Left:

Longitudinal cross-section of the Church of Saint-Louis des Invalides

François Lucas (ca. 1715-?) after Jean-Michel Chevotet (1698-1772) Etching and engraving, ca. 1736

Musée de l'Armée, Paris

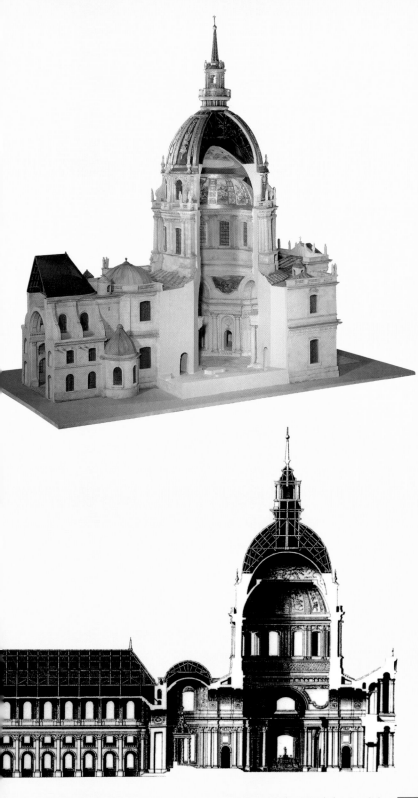

II.

The Church of the Dome and Napoleon's Tomb

Preceding pages:

Saint-Louis in glory, presenting arms to Christ in the presence of the Virgin and angels (detail)

Charles de La Fosse (1636-1716) Fresco, oil on plaster, 1702-1705, cupola of the Church of the Dome

Left:

The tomb of Napoleon I in the Church of the Dome

A complex history

Originally a royal church, the Church of the Dome extolled the glory of the French monarchy, of Louis XIV, and of his armies.
The décor and the architectural plan of the monument seek to celebrate the King of France's legitimacy as the representative of God on Earth, defender of the Catholic faith, and heir to the oldest throne of Europe.
During the Revolution, starting in 1792-1793, the Church of the Invalides was closed to services and transformed into a "Temple of Victory" and then a "Temple of Mars".
When Napoleon Bonaparte came to power, initially as First Consul and then as Emperor, he re-established the religious function of the church of the Invalides, but he also used the Church of the Dome to house the tombs of the great military personalities of France: Maréchal de Turenne in 1800, and Maréchal de Vauban in 1808.
In 1840, when the remains of Napoleon I were repatriated, Louis-Philippe's regime decided that the Emperor's grave should be placed beneath the Dome. This monumental tomb, completed in 1861 after twenty years of work and unexpected

obstacles, transformed its new setting in an open "crypt" at the church's transept, whose décor celebrates the glory of the Emperor.

The Church of the Dome was thus confirmed as a military pantheon centered upon the great figure of Napoleon I. But it also functioned as a pantheon of the imperial dynasty when Napoleon I's nephew, the Emperor Napoleon III, had the tombs of two of the Emperor's brothers, Joseph Bonaparte, King of Naples and, later, of Spain, and Jérôme Bonaparte, King of Westphalia, installed there. Later on, the Republic continued to honor its most prestigious military chiefs by welcoming their remains in the church of the Invalides. Following the victory over Germany in 1918, the Third Republic reinforced the tradition of the hôtel of the Invalides as a military pantheon. In 1929, a law was voted to this effect, and the government decided to place the tomb of Maréchal Foch beneath the Dome. The Fifth Republic gave Maréchal Lyautey his final resting place there as well.

The Exterior of the Church:
the Power of a Royal Edifice

The lower part of the Church of the Dome forms a huge, quadrangular pillar upon a flat-surfaced socle, which is surmounted by a very high, domed drum that measures 101.34 meters at its highest point (the tip of the cross). The volume and the vertical momentum of the building provide a striking contrast to the long and low nave of the Soldiers' Church.

• The facade

It consists of a salient facade of two stories of columns and pilasters, the lower Doric, the upper Corinthian, originally decorated by an ensemble of statues, a few of which remain. François Girardon initiated this sculpted pattern, complement to that of the interior of the church, in about 1690-1691, until he retired in 1700. The work then resumed under his successor, Antoine Coysevox, assisted by his nephew, Nicolas Coustou, at the beginning of the 18th century. Two statues of the patron saints of the French royal dynasty, *Charlemagne*, by Coysevox, on the left and *Saint Louis*, holding the Crown of Thorns, on the right, by Nicolas Coustou, frame the monumental door to the church in recesses on both sides.

At the second story, the four figures of the cardinal virtues–*Force, Justice, Temperance* and *Prudence*–are the work of Pierre Mazeline, and the chutes of trophies of arms held by angels are the work of Pierre Legros.

The pediment at the top is stamped with the coat of arms of France, and on the cornice, a series of large figures represented other virtues, as well as the fathers of the Latin and Greek churches. Sixteen other figures of apostles and saints, which have also disappeared, once graced the balustrade that separates the two stories of windows from the dome.

Scale model of the Church of the Dome, from the south façade

Philippe Velu, 1997

Musée de l'Armée, Paris

• *The dome*

The dome is embellished with a great lambrequin and chutes of trophies of arms in lead that were gilded in 1691-1692. It has been restored, including renewal of the gold leaf, on several occasions, in 1807, between 1866 and 1869, in 1936-1937, and, most recently, from 1988 to 1989. This last time, 12.65 kilos of gold, or some 550,000 gold leaves, were required to restore a total surface of 1850 square meters.

The lantern of the cupola is surmounted by a spire decorated with fleur de lys carrying a globe topped with a cross and four figures of gilded lead representing the divine virtues–*Faith, Charity,* and *Hope*–accompanied by *Religion,* the ensemble restored only recently (1989).

Lambrequin of the dome, holding trophies of arms (detail)

Lantern of the dome (detail)

The dome, seen from the southwest

• *The door*

The great portal of the church, once painted in white and gold, is richly sculpted with a pattern of fleur de lys and stamped with the coat of arms and the king's monogram, two interlaced "L" s.

Visit

The visit of the Church of the Dome can be organised into three great spatial ensembles:

• *at the center, and above,* the double cupola and the pendentives, with their painted and sculpted décor.

• *at a man's height,* the six chapels (4 corner chapels and 2 median chapels) and the choir.

• *below,* the great central excavation in which Napoleon's tomb lies.

Church of the Dome, from the "crypt" to the cupola

The Interior of the Church: Three Great Spatial Ensembles

The church, which is 55 meters long, is built in the form of a Greek cross, with four arms of equal length branching out from the central rotunda. The walls are marked with a series of majestic columns and pilasters in Corinthian style, the most ornate of the orders, symbolizing royalty. The impressive entablature that circles the interior of the building is marked with Louis XIV's monogram, which is repeated upon the groins of the vaults, accompanied by a radiant sun and fleur de lys.

The choir, the main altar and its canopy

These symbols of the monarchy can be found on the church floor as well, executed in a mosaic of colored marble, the central portion of which was removed during the work to hollow out the excavation. Most of these symbols were eliminated during the Revolution and then re-established when the Bourbons returned to the throne during the Restoration.

Between 1677 and 1690, there were several plans for the paintings and sculptures to decorate the vaults and cupolas of the church. In 1700, the entirety of the painted décor was divided up between Charles de La Fosse and several of his colleagues, Noël Coypel, Jean Jouvenet, Michel II Corneille, the brothers Bon and Louis de Boullogne, and Charles-François Poërson. The paintings, begun in 1702, were nearly all finished by 1704, some of them painted in fresco, others on a dry surface, a combination due to the difficulty of French artists in mastering the complex technique of the fresco.

The Transept, Cupolas and Pendentives: the Blending of the Throne and the Altar

The paintings and sculptures that decorate the transept, the double cupola, and the pendentives evoke themes defined during the reign of Louis XIV and celebrate the Catholic religion, whose greatest protector was presented as the King of France. In addition to the apostles and the evangelists, intermediaries between God and man, the patron saint of the church, Saint Louis, is honored in a series of bas reliefs that relate episodes of his life and by his presence at the feet of Christ in the painting on the upper cupola. He represents the special bond between the French monarchy and God.

• *The transept*

At the angles of the ribs of the vault, columns with wide entablatures frame the accesses to the four corner chapels. The arches of these passages are surmounted by great bas reliefs, dating from 1701, that show angels holding the symbols of the religious and warrior monarchy: the fleur de lys banner (Corneille Van Cleve), the ampulla [a phial of holy oil used to anoint the kings of France during their consecration] (Anselme Flamen), the shield with the coat of arms of France (Nicolas Coustou), and the royal helmet (Antoine Coysevox).

Angel holding the Ampulla

Anselme Flamen
(1647-1717)
Haut-relief above
the entrance to one
of the chapels, 1701

Sculptures in relief retracing the life of Saint Louis crown the other entrances to these chapels.

Above the entablatures, the pendentives of the drum are decorated with large paintings of the evangelists (*Saints Matthew, Mark, Luke* and *John*) by Charles de La Fosse. Higher up, at the base of the drum, a band patterned with fleurs de lys is stamped with the likenesses of the principal kings of France, from Clovis to Louis XIV (redone after 1815). It meets the pilasters separating the twelve windows.

Saint Mark the Evangelist

Charles de La Fosse (1636-1716)
Painting of one of the pendentives of the cupola, 1702-1705

• *The cupola*

Above the cornice rises a cupola, sectioned by bands of golden casings into compartments painted with ethereal figures of the apostles by Jean Jouvenet.

From the ground floor of the church, it is impossible to perceive the space that separates the open cupola (the opening is 14.65 meters in diameter), from the closed one which surmounts it. The latter is adorned with La Fosse's great painting, *Saint Louis in glory, presenting arms to Christ in the presence of the Virgin and the angels (1702-1705)*.

The composition celebrates the victory of the Catholic religion over the heathens, the triumph of orthodoxy over heresy.

Following pages:

The cupola of the Church of the Dome

Coupe et elevation   geometrale du Dôme.

*Cross section and geometric
erection of the dome*

François Lucas (ca. 1715?),
after Jean-Michel Chevotet (1698-1772)
Etching and engraving, ca. 1736

Musée de l'Armée, Paris

Following page:

Inside the dome, the open lower cupola
is surmounted by the closed upper
cupola, decorated with the paintings
of Charles de La Fosse.

The Double Cupola of the Dome of the Invalides

In his 1676-1677 plans for the Church of the Dome, Jules Hardouin-Mansart had originally imagined a traditional cupola of one sole piece. But when construction began, in 1687, he decided on a different design, inspired by the plans François Mansart, his famous grand-uncle, had drawn in the 1660s for the Bourbon chapel at Saint-Denis. The new cupola was double.

Only one of the two stories of windows visible at the exterior of the drum would be apparent from the interior. The first level of windows would allow abundant light inside the drum and the first cupola, the inferior one, open at the center to permit a view of the second, superior cupola.

This second cupola, completely closed at its summit, would capture the light of day through its second level of windows, visible from the exterior. La Fosse's aerial composition covering it is brightened particularly by the sun's reflection on the flat, stone roofs of the lower part of the church.

Apart from this very new architectural aspect, the construction of two cupolas, entirely in freestone, and the difficult bias carving of high stone window frames constitute a remarkable tour de force.

The engraving of François Lucas and Jean Michel Chevotet perfectly illustrates the articulation of these two superimposed cupolas which are surmounted by an important structure supporting the lantern and its spire.

The soaring erection of the royal church and the technical audacity of its construction are proof of the architect's ambition, the competence of his atelier of assistants, and the expertise of the masons he employed.

The Dome, begun in 1687, was covered in 1690. The lantern and its corona were mounted in 1691.

The Choir and the Chapels, from Liturgical Function to the Marshals of the Republic

Following pages:

The vault of the choir with the paintings of Noël Coypel, *The Holy Trinity* and, behind the upper canopy, *The Assumption of the Virgin*, 1702-1704

At right:

The choir, with the main altar surmounted by the canopy by Louis Visconti (1791-1853)

Below:

The banister of the stairway leading to the main altar

• *The choir and the altar*

Mansart's altar (1705-1708) was double, the lower part turned toward the Soldiers' Church, the other, higher, toward the dome, surmounted by a large canopy with six columns, decorated with scrolls and great figures of angels. Destroyed during the Revolution, the altar and the baldaquin were restored by the architect Louis Visconti when work was undertaken to install the Emperor's tomb, between 1842 and 1853.

The new canopy, directly inspired by that of Bernini in Saint Peter's Basilica in Rome, larger and more massive than Mansart's, is supported by four, 7-meter-high, cabled columns of Saint-Girons marble in black veined with white. The voluted entablature, decorated with angels carrying a cartouche that bears the monogram SL (Saint-Louis) is surmounted by a globe and a cross. Above the altar is a large, bronze Christ, the work of Henri de Triqueti.

At the vault, Noël Coypel painted *The Holy Trinity in Glory* above the baldaquin and *The Assumption of the Virgin* in the cul-de-four of the apse, both between 1702 and 1704.

PLAN GENERALE DE L'EGLISE ROYALE DES INVALIDES.

88

• *The four corner chapels and the two median chapels*

These six chapels are dedicated to the Virgin and great figures of the Roman Catholic church.
The corner chapels, devoted to the fathers of the Church, are round, embellished with elaborate Corinthian columns, and contain recesses designed to receive imposing statues of the titular saint and two of his disciples. The vault is divided into six paintings that tell the story of the life of each respective saint, with his ascent into heaven represented in the calotte. The median chapels are dedicated to the Virgin and Saint Theresa (probably as a flattering reference to the Spanish spouse of Louis XIV, Marie-Thérèse d'Autriche, who died in 1683).
The role of these chapels, whose furnishings were confiscated during the Revolution, changed in the 19th and the 20th centuries. Their use as the scene for funeral monuments replaced their religious vocation.
☞ Going clockwise, the first chapel, at the left of the entry, is consecrated to Saint-Jérôme.

Marble mosaic of the pavement of the Church of the Dome: the crowned great arms of France lie at the center of large necklaces of the two royal orders of Saint-Michel (created in 1469) and Saint-Louis (established in 1693).

Lespingola, Fontenoy and Audran, 1701-1709

The Chapel of Saint-Jérôme

The paintings are the work of Bon Boullogne (1702-1704). From the return of the remains until 1861, during the excavation work at the transept crossing of the Church of the Dome, the casket of Napoleon I was kept in the chapel of Saint-Jérôme.

In 1861, architect Alfred-Nicolas Normand began the work to place the tomb of Napoleon's youngest brother, King Jérôme (1784-1860), King of Westphalia (1807-1814) and Governor of the Invalides from 1848 to 1853, in the chapel. He was interred there in 1862. His tomb is surmounted by his statue, the work of Eugène Guillaume.

An urn in the form of an antique altar holding the heart of his wife, Queen Catherine of Wurtemberg (1783-1835), stands in the central recess, while the casket of their eldest son, Prince Jérôme (1814-1847), lies in the vault beneath the chapel, along with the urn that contains the heart of Général Leclerc (1772-1802) the first husband of the Emperor's sister Pauline Bonaparte.

Left:

Visit of Queen Victoria to the Invalides, August 24th, 1855
During her visit to Paris on the occasion of the Universal Exposition of 1855, Queen Victoria and her husband, Prince Albert, arrive at the Invalides to honor the memory of the Emperor, whose casket is displayed in the Chapel of Saint-Jérôme.

Paul-Emile Boutigny
(1854-1930)
Oil on canvas

Musée de l'Armée, Paris

Above:

The cupola of the Chapel of Saint-Jérôme with *The Life and Glory of Saint-Jérôme* by Bon Boullogne, 1702-1704

The Chapel of the Virgin

The former Chapel of the Virgin lost its altar and its statues.

As First Consul, Napoleon was the first political chief to choose the Dome as the grandiose setting of a memorial to the military glory of the past. In 1800, he decided to have the remains of Turenne (1611-1675), one of France's finest marshals of *le grand siècle,* who had been buried, in an act of exceptional favor, at the necropolis of the kings of France at Saint-Denis by order of Louis XIV, transferred to the Invalides. His funeral monument, spared profanation during the Revolution, was erected beneath the dome. Lazare Carnot, Minister of War, explained this decision in his speech of September 22, 1800. Known for his integrity, his loyalty, and his devotion to the country, it was natural that Turenne should lie in peace at the Invalides, among deserving old soldiers. *"The ashes of the brave belong to the brave; they are the natural guardians, they should cherish this charge."* Turenne's monument, executed shortly after his death, is the work of sculptors Jean-Baptiste Tuby

Tomb of Maréchal Turenne, Chapel of the Virgin

Jean-Baptiste Tuby (1635-1700) and Gaspard Marsy (1624-1681) Marble and bronze, ca. 1675-1680

and Gaspard Marsy. The Maréchal lies across the remains of a lion, like a latter day Hercules, brandishing his baton of command, and leaning against the knees of *Immortality*, who holds the victor's laurel wreath. The eagle of the German Empire he has fought so often is seen flying away in terror.

Upon the sarcophagus, a bronze bas relief depicts the battle of Turckheim in which Turenne won fame in 1675, a few months before his death. On one side and the other, two figures mourn the loss of their defender: on the left, *Wisdom*, leaning upon an altar and some books, holding a vase that pours out pieces of money, symbolizing the hero's generosity; on the right, a helmeted figure of *Valor*, seated upon weapons. An obelisk, symbolizing eternity, surmounts the monument.

ETRE DE CEUX AUXQUELS
LES HOMMES CROIENT DANS
LES YEUX DESQUELS DES
MILLIERS D'YEUX CHERCHENT

LORDRE A LA VOIX DESQUELS
DES ROUTES S'OUVRENT
DES PAYS SE PEUPLENT
DES VILLES SURGISSENT

The Chapel of Saint-Grégoire

In 1764, Carle Van Loo was commissioned to redo the painted décor of Michel II Corneille, ruined by humidity during the 18th century, but it was Gabriel Doyen who did the actual work, between 1765 and 1771.

The original statues have disappeared and were replaced by a *Christ Resurrected* by Michel-Ange Slodtz (1736), as well as a figure

representing *Religion*, by Pierre Mazeline and Simon Hurtrel (1688), originally from the tomb of Charles III, Duc de Créqui, in the destroyed church of the Capucines.

In the central recess, an urn contains the heart of Théophile-Malo Corret de La Tour d'Auvergne (1743-1800), "First Grenadier of the Republic", hero of the Revolutionary wars.

The tomb of Maréchal Lyautey (1854-1934) was placed at the center of the chapel. His presence is due to his fame as Résident General of France in Morocco from 1912 to 1925. In this position, Lyautey showed himself to be a remarkable administrator, contributing to the modernisation of Morocco while respecting its traditions. Général de Gaulle had Lyautey's remains returned from Morocco in 1961, thus symbolically marking an end to the colonial era.

Lyautey's funeral monument, the work of Albert Laprade, was placed in the chapel in 1963. It consists of a bronze sarcophagus mounted upon marble supports and bears two inscriptions; one in Arabic, the other in French. The first, taken from Lyautey's correspondence as a young man, resumés the marshal's work: "*I thought I could be one of those in whom men could believe, in whose eyes thousands of eyes sought order, whose voice could cause roads to open, countries to repopulate, cities to emerge.*" The inscription in Arabic evokes Lyautey's attachment to Morocco: "*The more I know the Moroccans and the longer I live in this country, the more I am convinced of the grandeur of this nation.*"

The Chapel of Saint-Ambroise

The paintings are the work of Bon Boullogne. The ornamental plaster statues that once adorned the altars and chapels of the church were gradually replaced by marble figures between 1748 and 1789. These were dismantled and sold during the Revolution, but two were returned to the church and placed here: *Sainte Paule,* by Christophe-Gabriel Allegrain and Louis-Philippe Mouchy (1768-1784) and *Sainte Eustochie* by Pierre-Etienne Monnot (1781-1782), which were originally in the chapel of Saint-Jérôme.

The casket of Maréchal Foch (1851-1929), the generalissimo who led the Allies to victory over Germany in 1918, was temporarily placed in the governors' vault in 1929, and then moved to the chapel of Saint-Ambroise.

The installation of the marshal's tomb there necessitated a modification of the marble mosaics of the floor. Now they display a pattern of stars, the names of Foch's victories, and his marshal's baton framed by two interlacing "F" s.

The funeral monument, sculpted by Paul Landowski, was inaugurated in 1937. It depicts French artillerymen carrying the marshal's remains on a bed of laurels. One side of the tomb, which is not visible to the public, is inscribed with the words "*Maréchal Foch (1851-1929)*", and depicts his three marshal's batons, of France, Great Britain, and Poland.

Opposite:

Tomb of Maréchal Foch, Chapel of Saint-Ambroise

Paul Landowski (1875-1961) Bronze, 1931-1937

Above:

*Detail
of the tomb:
Science* and
Vauban

Tomb of
Maréchal
Vauban, Chapel
of Saint-Thérèse

Antoine Etex
(1808-1888)
Marble, 1846-1847

VAUBAN

The Chapel of Sainte-Thérèse

The former chapel of Sainte-Thérèse was transformed when Maréchal de Vauban's funeral monument was installed in 1846-1847.

In 1808, after Turenne was placed in the chapel of the Virgin, perhaps with respect for historical symmetry in mind, Napoleon decided to install the heart of Vauban in the chapel of Sainte-Thérèse. Like Turenne, Maréchal de Vauban (1633-1707) was a great servant of the nation. Moderniser of the fortifications of France's borders, he is considered a model of the disinterested patriot, *"perhaps the most honest and virtuous of his century."* (Saint Simon). He is the author of a *Project for a Royal Tithe,* which proposed a tax to be paid by all. The project was made public in 1707 and disclaimed by Louis XIV and his ministers. Legend has it that the aged Vauban, his integrity intact, died in disgrace of a broken heart, a martyr to the cause of the struggle against privilege.

The first funeral monument, by Guillaume Trepsat, the architect of the hôtel, consisted of a column surmounted by an urn containing the heart of Vauban.

Under Louis-Philippe, during work on Napoleon's tomb and with an eye to symmetry, Trepsat's monument was replaced by another that resembled Turenne's. The work of Antoine Etex, it was placed under the Dome in 1847.

A semi-reclining Vauban, leaning on several volumes of his works and holding a compass, meditates upon his own writings. A veiled figure of *Science* and one of *War,* wearing a helmet, flank the marshal at the foot of a great obelisk surrounded by flags and standards.

An inscription in bas-relief on the plinth evokes the project of the royal tithe and emphasizes the political and reforming dimensions of Vauban's work.

The Chapel of Saint-Augustin

Its paintings are the work of Louis de Boullogne.

Like those of the other corner chapels, they depict the major episodes in the life of Saint Augustine and his ascension into Heaven.

All of the original statues have disappeared, replaced in the 19th century by a figure of *Religion*, sculpted by Jacques Bousseau in 1736 for the salon of the chapel of the château of Versailles, but never actually installed there ; and Mazeline and Hurtrel's 1688 sculpture, *Abundance*, which comes from the tomb of the Duc de Créqui at the Capucine church.

In 1864, at the instigation of Emperor Napoleon III and by stretching the terms of the 1840 law consecrating the entirety of the church to the sepulture of Napoleon I, the tomb of Joseph Bonaparte (1768-1844), Napoleon's older brother, was placed at the center of the chapel. King of Naples (1806-1808), and then of Spain (1808-1813), he left France in 1815 when Napoleon fell, living first in the United States, then in Great Britain, and finally in Italy. He died in Florence. His sarcophaghus of black marble veined with white was made by Crépinet in 1863-1864.

The Life and Glory of Saint Augustine

Louis de Boullogne
(1654-1733)
Cupola of the
Chapel of Saint-
Augustin
(1702-1706)

Left:

The tomb
of Joseph
Bonaparte
(1768-1844) in
the Chapel of
Saint-Augustin

Crépinet
Marble, 1863-1864

The Great Central Excavation: Napoleon's Tomb

Preceding pages:

Arrival of the cortege and the funereal chariot bearing Napoleon I at the Invalides, December 15th, 1840

Anonymous
Oil on canvas, ca. 1840

Musée Carnavalet, Paris

Today the Dome is famous as the shelter of the tomb of Napoleon I. The site was chosen in 1840 by King Louis-Philippe and his Président du conseil [government head], Adolphe Thiers. The return of the Emperor's remains, accepted by the British and announced by Minister of the Interior Charles de Rémusat on May 12, 1840, was a move designed to please the public and prove that the regime was capable of reconciling the French with their history. The official reasons for placing Napoleon's tomb at the Invalides were the same as those that applied to Turenne: the Invalides is a temple of military glory, watched over by deserving old soldiers, and Napoleon's tomb should naturally be a part of it.

This decision resulted in the law of June 10, 1840, stipulating that *"The tomb shall be placed beneath the dome, consecrated, as well as the four lateral chapels [the corner chapels], to the sepulture of the Emperor Napoleon."* The Prince de Joinville, son of Louis-Philippe, was charged with the mission of bringing the body of Napoleon back to France from the island of Saint Helena. On December 15, 1840, in a grandiose ceremony, the sovereign welcomed the remains of the Emperor to the Invalides.

In 1841, the committee judging the competition of different projects submitted for funeral monuments chose that of Louis-Tullius-Joachim Visconti, a naturalised French citizen of Italian origin, who had organised the official Return of the Remains ceremonies in 1840. He proposed that a space below be excavated to house the tomb, and it was deemed that this plan was the one that would least mar the architectural harmony of the church.

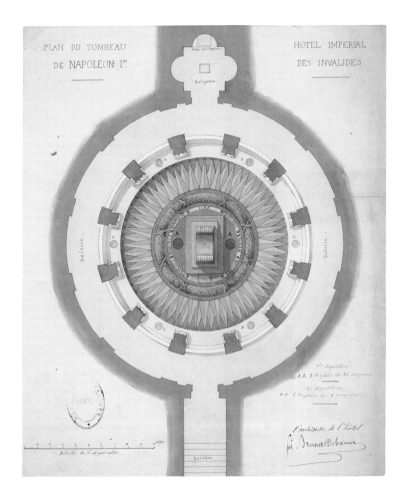

The installation of the tomb entailed some major architectural revisions: an excavation 6 meters deep and 15 meters in diameter (21 meters, including the circulation gallery) was hollowed out at the transept crossing. The work, often delayed by political changes, in particular the Revolution of 1848, dragged on and proved more costly than initially expected. When Visconti died, in 1853, the ensemble was nearly complete, but the inauguration and the transfer of Napoleon's remains from the Chapel of Saint Jérôme to the new tomb did not take place until April 2, 1861, under the Second Empire.

Plan for the crypt and the tomb
Alfred Louis Brunet-Debaines (1845-1939)
Aquarelle, 1861
Musée de l'Armée, Paris

JE·DÉSIRE·QUE·MES·CENDRES·REPOSENT
SUR·LES·BORDS·DE·LA·SEINE
AU·MILIEU·DE·CE·PEUPLE·FRANÇAIS
QUE·J'AI·TANT·AIMÉ.

Access to the Tomb

Two stairways, situated at either side of the main altar, lead to the excavation. Marble marquetterie has been reinstalled at the bottom of the stairs, where the emblem of Louis XIV has been replaced by the crowned "N" of Napoleon.

On opposite sides of the window that has separated the Church of the Dome from the Soldiers' Church since 1873 are the funeral monuments of Général Duroc (1772-1813), Grand Maréchal du Palais, mortally wounded at Bautzen, and of Général Bertrand (1773-1844), Grand Maréchal du Palais, his successor, faithful among the faithful at Saint Helena. Also designed by Visconti, both of these tombs received the remains of their generals in 1847.

The monumental bronze door that opens on to the stairs descending to the tomb is flanked by two colossal bronze figures of funerary spirits, veiled and crowned with cypress, by Joseph Duret. They bear the symbols of imperial power on a cushion: one, the crown and the hand of justice, the other, the sword and the globe.

An inscription taken from the Emperor's will is graven on the tympan, above the door: « *It is my wish that my remains repose on the banks of the Seine, amidst the French people, whom I have loved so well* ». The allusion is vague, nonetheless it justifies the choice of the Invalides as the site of the Emperor's sepulture rather than Saint Denis Basilica, the ancient necropolis of French sovereigns, where he had thought of being buried.

At the foot of the stairs, at the right, in the vestibule, a bronze door leads to the vault where Maréchal Mortier, Duc de Trévise, lies in repose, along with thirteen other victims of the July 28, 1835, Fieschi plot to assassinate King Louis-Philippe.

On either side of the vestibule, white marble bas-reliefs depict, on the left, *The Prince de Joinville and his travel companions meditating at Napoleon's tomb at Saint Helena,* by Augustin Dumont, and, at the right, *The prince delivering the remains of the Emperor to his father, King Louis-Philippe, in the church of the Invalides*, by François Jouffroy. Completed in 1851, these bas-reliefs were not installed until 1910.

Entry to the "crypt", designed by Louis Visconti (1791-1853, with the *Funerary Spirits* by Joseph Duret (1804-1865)

The Tomb: an Imperial Program

The "crypt", with the tomb of Napoleon I.

Right:

The Creation of the Council of State Charles Simart (1806-1857) Haut-relief (1846-1853) of the circular gallery of the "crypt"

Upon entering the excavation, the eye is immediately drawn to the sarcophagus. Napoleon's tomb was originally planned in porphyry of purple, the color reserved for emperors since Antiquity. Unable to find a sufficient quantity of such material on French soil, engineer Louis Léouzon-Leduc was sent on an exploratory mission which led him to Russia, a country rich in rare and precious stone. At the end of a long search, he found an aventurine quartzite of a color and density comparable to that of porphyry on an island in Lake Onega. Acquired from the czar, the blocks were transported to Paris by ship and carved using a steam-powered machine custom conceived and constructed by engineer and monument mason Antoine Séguin.

The Emperor's sarcophagus is nearly 4 meters long and over 2 meters wide and consists of a great ark adorned with laurel wreaths, closed by a scrolled cover. It rests upon a socle of green granite from the Vosges, the entire ensemble nearly 5 meters high. The interior of the ark is lined in lilac Corsican marble.

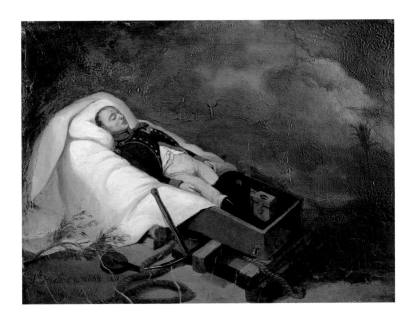

The Emperor's caskets

Napoleon I in his coffin at the moment of the exhumation on the island of Saint Helena, October 15th, 1840
Henri-Daniel Plattel (1803-1859)
Oil on canvas, ca. 1840
Musée de l'Armée, Paris

Napoleon I at Fontainebleau, March 31, 1814
Paul Delaroche (1797-1856)
Oil on canvas, 1840
Musée de l'Armée, Paris

The Emperor was placed inside the sarcophagus on April 2, 1861, enclosed in five coffins that fit one into the other (tin, two of lead, ebony and oak). He is dressed in the green uniform of a colonel of the cavalry of the Imperial Guard and wears on his breast the sash, the insignia, and the cross of the Legion of Honor as well as the cross of the Order of the Iron Crown.

One of his legendary hats lies on his legs, and silver boxes containing his heart and his viscera are placed at his feet.

If the tomb itself bears no inscription, the ensemble of the surrounding décor is evocative of the memory of Napoleon.

Twelve colossal marble figures of *Victory*, bearing laurel wreaths and palms, recall the triumphant campaigns of the Emperor. Massive and severe, 4.50 meters high, they are the work of James Pradier.

On the ground, a polychrome mosaic depicting a star within a crown of laurels enumerates Napoleon's eight most famous victories: Rivoli (1797), the Pyramids (1798), Marengo (1800), Austerlitz (1805), Iéna (1806), Friedland (1807), Wagram (1809), and Moskowa (1812).

The circular gallery and the cella

The ten white marble haut-reliefs of the circular gallery, sculpted by Charles Simart, represent Napoleon's civil achievements. On the left, the first five celebrate Napoleon, draped in a costume of Antiquity, as protector of the State who rebuilt society on new foundations: *the pacification of civic unrest, administrative centralisation, the Council of State, the Civil Code,* (known as the Code Napoleon from 1807 on), *the Concordat.*

The gallery with its coffered ceiling, lit by large bronze lamps in antique style, leads to a cella facing the entry. This was once called a reliquary for it then contained some of the most precious souvenirs of the Emperor, conserved today at the Musée de l'Armée.

A 2.60 meter statue by Simart, of white marble, accented with gold, portrays Napoleon I in coronation costume, leaning on the sceptre and bearing the globe with the cross. The statue rises over the tombstone of the Aiglon.

The names of Napoleon's many victories are engraved upon the walls.

Simart's five other bas-reliefs follow. They exalt Napoleon as the man who, once he had reformed society, knew how to make it function: *the University, the Government Accounting Office, Industry and Commerce, the major projects, the Legion of Honor.* In this vision that combines history and legend, Napoleon emerges as a talented administrator who guaranteed order and prosperity, author of the synthesis between the Ancien Régime and the Revolution.

Following pages:
The Hôtel des Invalides and the Quartermaster's garden, seen from the south west

The tomb of the Aiglon

In the cella, at the foot of the statue of Napoleon II, a stone bears the inscription "Napoleon II, King of Rome, 1811-1832". The son of Napoleon and Marie-Louise who, after his father fell from power, lived in Austria and held the title of Duc de Reichstadt, was buried in the crypt of the Capucines in Vienna, necropolis of the Hapsburg dynasty. His remains were returned to France by Germany in 1940 and laid to rest at the Invalides on December 15. Having lain in the chapel of Saint-Jérôme for a time, the bronze casket of the Aiglon was finally placed in a crypt beneath the cella in 1969.

Statue of Napoleon I by Charles Simart and tombstone of Napoleon II, King of Rome. Cella, circular gallery

III.

The Hospital Buildings and Gardens

When he designed the church of the Dome, Jules Hardouin-Mansart thought of creating a royal square before it, with two grand colonnades in an arc, (see p. 120) similar to the square Louis Le Vau created before the Collège des Quatre Nations, today the Institut de France, recalling Bernini's esplanade before Saint Peter's Basilica in Rome.
This grandiose project never saw the light of day.

Opposite:

Child apothecaries
Jacques Verberckt (1704-1771)
Cartouche of the paneling (1736-1737) of the former pharmacy of the Hôtel des Invalides, the present day conference room of the Institution nationale des Invalides.

☞ The visit is complete on leaving the Church of the Dome to explore the south section of the Hôtel des Invalides.

L'Institution nationale des Invalides

On either side of the Church of the Dome, the visitor can glimpse the long, low buildings occupied today by the Institution nationale des Invalides.
Placed under the authority of the Governor of the Invalides, an important military figure, and of a surgeon general, the INI (Institution nationale des Invalides) affirms the persistence of the initial vocation of the Invalides up to the present day. The establishment includes a hospital section, a medico-surgical section (known for its excellent care, particularly in the domain of war wounds), and a retirement home that welcomes veterans, the direct heirs of the residents of the Hôtel in the days when it was created.

On the east–the present-day hospital (reserved access)–are the infirmaries, built in 1679, and the former bakery, constructed in the 18th century. On the west–where the (reserved access) resthome is currently located–the workshops, completed in 1691, open out on to the Quartermasters' garden.

The Quartermasters garden

Recreated in the years 1970 to 1980 around an ornamental pond, it contains the memorial fountain, *Parole portée*, by Nicolas Alquin (1998), dedicated to the victims of terrorist attacks who are now welcomed, in the same capacity as the war invalids, in the premises of the Institution nationale des Invalides. On the west, along the Boulevard Latour-Maubourg, Jules-Robert de Cotte built an extension to the building in 1749, intended as a residence of the officers of the hotel. Today it houses the chancellery and the Musée de l'Ordre de la Libération.

Buildings of the Institution nationale des Invalides and the Church of the Dome

19th century pharmacy (Institution nationale des Invalides)

So ends the visit of the Hôtel National des Invalides, a remarkable architectural ensemble of the century of Louis XIV. Initially dedicated to housing wounded soldiers, it retains its mission even today. Since the 19th century, it has progressively become France's military pantheon as well, and the national conservatory of the collections linked to the military history of the country.

For further study

Contemporary sources

Le Jeune de Boulencourt, *Description générale de l'Hostel royal des Invalides,* Paris, 1683.

J. F. Félibien des Avaux, *Description de l'Eglise royale des Invalides,* Paris, 1706.

J.-J. Granet, *Histoire de l'Hôtel royal des Invalides,* Paris, 1736.

G. Pérau, *Description historique de l'Hôtel royal des Invalides,* Paris, 1756; reprinted by B. Jestaz, Paris/Geneva, 1974.

Recent publications

Editorial collective, *Les Invalides, trois siècles d'histoire* (Paris: Musée de l'Armée), 1974.

A. Muratori-Philip, *Les Grandes Heures des Invalides* (Paris: Perrin), 1989.

J.-P. Bois, *Les Anciens Soldats dans la société française au XVIIIe siècle* (Paris: Economica), 1990.

B. Jestaz, *L'Hôtel et l'église des Invalides* (Paris: CNMHS/Picard), 1990.

Napoleon aux Invalides, 1840, le retour des Cendres (exhibition catalogue) (Paris: Musée de l'Armée), 1990.

J. Dorland, *L'Hôtel des Invalides, son service de santé, son hôpital, ses pensionnaires, de Louis XIV à nos jours* (Paris: J. Dorland), 1996.

preceding pages:
The Hôtel des Invalides with the colonnades designed by Jules Hardouin-Mansart, which were never actually installed. Anonymous engraving taken from J.-F. Félibien des Avaux, *Description de l'Église royale des Invalides,* Paris, 1706

Index

Index

Summary

The guide 47

PHOTOS CREDITS

Graphic conception: Bleu T
Secretary: Julie Houis
Translation: Jane Lizop
Translation editing: Carol Leimroth
Editing: Catherine Ojalvo
Fabrication: Audrey Chenu, Vincent Benzi, Saint-Véron Pompée

This work has been printed in Garamond and Formata
Paper: Satimat 135 g

Ouvrage publié avec le soutien de la Fondation EDF

Photogravure: Fotimprim, Paris

Printing and binding: Mame, Tours
Imprimerie Mame, Tours, May 2003

Diffusion Actes Sud
Distribution UD-Union Distribution
AS 0034

ISBN 2-87900-800-X
ISSN pending
Dépôt légal : mai 2003

Cover: *in* Guide pp. 44-45 and p. 110